About the Author

Sam holds a degree in Economics and Management from Oxford, an MSc in Economics from UCL and an Executive MBA from Warwick. He has over a decade's experience in financial services and is an experienced people manager who enjoys helping others to reach their potential.

Sam has written extensively for his university degrees and in his professional life, but this is his debut non-fiction work. It draws on his sense of humour, life experience, creativity and philosophical outlook on life.

Sam lives in London and in his spare time enjoys travelling and hiking. More recently Sam has performed his first stand-up comedy gig!

Sam Boundy

TWO MICE

A simple story about finding your way in a complicated world

AUSTIN MACAULEY PUBLISHERS™
LONDON · CAMBRIDGE · NEW YORK · SHARJAH

Copyright © Sam Boundy 2022
Illustrations © Sam Boundy 2022

The right of Sam Boundy to be identified as author of this work has been asserted by the author in accordance with sections 77 and 78 of the Copyright, Designs and Patents Act 1988.

All rights reserved. No part of this publication may be reproduced, stored in a retrieval system, or transmitted in any form or by any means, electronic, mechanical, photocopying, recording, or otherwise, without the prior permission of the publishers.

Any person who commits any unauthorised act in relation to this publication may be liable to criminal prosecution and civil claims for damages.

A CIP catalogue record for this title is available from the British Library.

ISBN 9781398486287 (Paperback)
ISBN 9781398486294 (ePub e-book)

www.austinmacauley.com

First Published 2022
Austin Macauley Publishers Ltd®
1 Canada Square
Canary Wharf
London
E14 5AA

Acknowledgements

I'd like to thank my friend Della for helping me in getting this work published. She tied my shoes for me when I was four and couldn't manage it myself. She's still helping me to this day, although thankfully now I can tie my own shoes!

The Lively Mouse and the Thoughtful Mouse

Once upon a time, in a faraway land, there lived two very similar mice. They grew up in the same village and had the same build, the same aptitude for problem-solving and the same hunger for cheese. The first mouse was a lively mouse who struggled to sit still and was always in a hurry. The second was a thoughtful mouse who listened intently to the other mice and would sit for hours thinking long and hard about what it all meant.

One day an old mouse from another village came and told the two mice a story about a very big cheese. The cheese, he told them, was so enormous that if they found it they would never go hungry again. It was the tastiest, most satisfying cheese in the entire land, but to find it they would have to leave their village and travel out into the big wide world.

'But where can we find this cheese?' asked the thoughtful mouse.

'If I knew that, do you think I'd be here,' scoffed the old mouse, 'of course I wouldn't. I'd be filling my belly with all that tasty cheese.'

'What can you tell us?' demanded the lively mouse, licking his lips in anticipation of a very big meal.

'I've spent my entire life searching for that cheese,' replied the old mouse, 'I've travelled further in the last year alone than many mice travel in a lifetime. I've come here from the West as far as my paws would carry me and I still haven't found that cheese!'

'Then I shall go North!' replied the lively mouse, before scurrying off on his merry way.

But that might be the wrong direction, worried the thoughtful mouse.

'Perhaps you could tell me more?' he said to the old mouse.

The two mice talked and talked as the sky turned to pink and then to orange and then to black. The old mouse told him the story of his entire life and shared with him all of its ups and downs. And as their tiny fire went out and they were illuminated just by starlight, the old mouse confided in the young mouse that somebody, somewhere had to know where that big cheese was and that if he found them and listened to them very carefully, he would eventually find it.

The Lively Mouse and the Clever Mouse

The lively mouse walked as far as he could while the sky turned to pink and then to orange and then to black. In those few hours, he travelled further from his village than he had ever been before, but he was in a hurry, the big cheese couldn't be far away. But perhaps he had scurried too fast, his paws were sore and blistered and his belly was rumbling.

He was relieved when he finally reached a small, thatched cottage with a tidy garden out front. He knocked on the door and waited impatiently for an answer.

The mouse that opened the door had untidy grey fur, a big round belly and spectacles coming down over his nose. He must be a very clever mouse, thought the lively mouse, noticing the book he was holding in his paw.

'What do you want at this late hour?' demanded the clever mouse.

'I am on a journey, to find a big cheese in a faraway land. But my paws are sore and I am hungry,' he explained. 'Can I stay here for a night? I will gladly do any odd jobs that you have for me.'

'Come in,' he replied, 'and tell me more about this big cheese. I'm having gouda for my tea which I will gladly share with you and then you can help me with my work tomorrow.'

'Thank you, sir,' said the lively mouse, 'I will work very hard for you tomorrow and then I will leave early the next day.'

The inside of the cottage was warm and cosy. There was a fire burning on the hearth and there was a very tasty-looking piece of gouda on the table by the fire. The room was full to bursting, however, with big, heavy books piled up as high as the ceiling against every wall.

'Why such a hurry?' asked the clever mouse, 'Please have some cheese and tell me about your journey.'

'Well sir,' explained the lively mouse, 'only today a mouse from another village visited and told us about a very big cheese in a faraway land and I am on an expedition to find it. It is the tastiest, most satisfying cheese there ever was and if I find it I will never go hungry again.'

'And do you know where this cheese is?' asked the clever mouse expectantly.

'No sir, but I'm sure if I keep searching I'll eventually find it,' the lively mouse replied hopefully.

'No, no, no,' scowled the clever mouse, 'you're going about this all wrong. You're going to get completely lost if you carry on like this. First off, you need to define the cheese. Does this cheese even exist, and if it does, is it a real cheese or a metaphysical cheese?'

'Please sir,' replied the lively mouse, 'I have travelled a long way and I am very tired. Perhaps we could discuss the work you have for me and then I could take an early night and get some rest.'

The clever mouse looked disappointed.

'I'm trying to help you,' he explained, 'I'm a professor and I have studied geography, philosophy, history and physics. If you want to find this big cheese of yours, don't you think you first need to understand everything we know about this land of ours, so you know where to look for this big cheese?'

'That sounds like an awful lot to understand,' sighed the lively mouse, 'I think I'd like to learn as I go. It will be an adventure.'

'As you wish,' replied the clever mouse dismissively.

'So what work do you have for me,' asked the lively mouse.

'You see this book on the table,' replied the clever mouse, 'it's my latest work. I need you to make as many copies as possible so that I can share it with the public.'

'Okay,' replied the lively mouse, 'now I will go to bed, but tomorrow, I will work very hard and make as many copies as I can.'

The lively mouse had only had a little schooling and his writing was slow and steady. But the next day he was up at the break of dawn and he worked harder than he had ever worked before. The first book took him an hour to copy, but the next one only fifty minutes and the next one was quicker again. He stopped only briefly for a quick mouthful of cheese and some water at lunchtime and worked faster and more efficiently as he went into the afternoon and then into the evening.

'You've worked very hard today,' said the clever mouse, 'and made many more copies of my book than I expected. Here is some cheese for your dinner and a little extra for you to take on your journey.'

'Thank you, sir,' said the lively mouse, 'I'm very grateful for your hospitality.'

'I do wish you would stay longer,' said the clever mouse, 'but I fear you have already made up your mind and tomorrow you will go.'

'Yes sir,' replied the lively mouse, 'I am on a journey and I mustn't stop, otherwise I really will get lost. But thank you once again for your kind hospitality.'

The clever mouse looked at him thoughtfully for a moment and then wished him good night. The lively mouse had a long journey ahead of him in the morning and needed to get some rest.

The Thoughtful Mouse and the Clever Mouse

The thoughtful mouse had been up late into the night talking about the big cheese and did not rise until late the next day. He too set off to the North and keen to make up for lost time, he scurried as fast as his little paws could carry him. After walking for many hours his paws were sore and blistered and his belly was rumbling.

He too came to a small, thatched cottage with a tidy garden out front.

He knocked on the door and waited for an answer.

'What do you want at this late hour?' demanded the clever mouse.

'I am on a journey, to find a big cheese in a faraway land. But my paws are sore and I am hungry.' He explained. 'Can I stay here for a night? I will gladly do any odd jobs that you have for me.'

'Come in,' he replied, 'and tell me more about this big cheese. I'm having gouda for my tea which I will gladly share with you and then you can help me with my work tomorrow.'

'Thank you, sir,' said the thoughtful mouse, 'I will work very hard for you tomorrow and would love to learn everything you can teach me about the big cheese.'

The clever mouse smiled a satisfied smile and showed the thoughtful mouse into his living room which was still full of books. There was a fire on the hearth and the same tasty piece of gouda on the table in front of it.

'So first,' explained the clever mouse, 'we need to define the cheese. We can't get anywhere, you see, without defining our terms.'

'I see,' said the thoughtful mouse, enjoying biting into his gouda while listening to what the clever mouse had to say.

The clever mouse found this response very encouraging.

'The first question,' he explained excitedly, 'is whether the big cheese is indeed an actual cheese or a metaphysical cheese.'

'Please sir,' asked the thoughtful mouse, 'what's a metaphysical cheese?'

'I'm glad you asked me that,' smiled the clever mouse, 'meta is Greek, it means with or after or sometimes beyond. It depends whether it's from the accusative or the genitive, if it's from the accusative it means beyond or after, if it's the genitive it means with, so in this case, metaphysical means beyond the physical realm.'

The thoughtful mouse was quiet for a long, long time while he contemplated what the clever mouse was saying.

'You mean the very big cheese isn't even real?' he demanded.

'Well, to answer that question we would have to define 'real' now wouldn't we?' smiled the clever mouse.

'Please sir,' begged the thoughtful mouse, 'you're clearly a very clever mouse, but I am only a simple mouse trying to find the very big cheese. I don't think I could ever understand as much as you, I'd just like you to help me find the big cheese.'

This seemed to please the clever mouse an awful lot. 'I'll tell you what,' said the clever mouse, 'if you help me with making copies of my book, you can stay here as long as you want and I will teach you everything that I know.'

The thoughtful mouse was quiet for even longer this time and thought long and hard about his decision. How was he going to find the big cheese if he stuck around here copying books? But then again, how was he going to find the big cheese if he didn't know anything about the world?

'I'll stay tomorrow and we can see how we get on,' the thoughtful mouse finally suggested, 'would that work for you, sir?'

'That will be fine,' smiled the clever mouse, 'I am a professor and I have studied geography, philosophy, history and physics. I have a lot to teach you and I am sure that once I have taught you, the very big cheese will make a lot more sense and be easily within your grasp.'

The next day the thoughtful mouse spent a long time talking with the clever mouse over breakfast and then again over lunch and dinner. He copied the clever mouse's book slowly, but carefully. He knew he could have worked faster, but the clever mouse didn't seem to mind and seemed most happy with him when they were talking.

They went on like this for days and then for months and then for years. The clever mouse taught him that the very big cheese the old mouse had told him about didn't have to be a real cheese like cheddar or brie, but could just as easily represent something else. 'But how,' the clever mouse regularly asked him, 'do we know that it is a cheese?'

The clever mouse taught him much philosophy, but just when the thoughtful mouse decided that any more philosophy couldn't really help him get any closer to finding the big cheese, the clever mouse had shifted tact, and started to teach him psychology.

'The cheese,' the clever mouse argued, 'is not a cheese at all, but a manifestation of our ego's longing for meaning in a meaningless world.'

'But if that's true,' the thoughtful mouse had asked, 'maybe I should stop all this studying and stop my search for the big cheese.'

'No,' the clever mouse had laughed, 'you don't understand, I'm not saying that the big cheese isn't a real cheese, I'm just saying that you need to look at the problem from every angle. Perhaps the big cheese does exist,' he had continued, before moving on to approach the problem scientifically.

'Let us take as our hypothesis that there is out there a big cheese, a real cheese that you can eat,' the clever mouse had explained, 'then what we need to do is design an experiment or a set of experiments that will enable you to find it.'

'I could go search for it,' said the thoughtful mouse.

'Yes,' said the clever mouse, 'but if you are going to do that, you will need to be methodological, use the process of elimination to understand where the cheese is not, so that you can pinpoint where the cheese is. And to do that, of course, I will have to teach you the scientific method.'

The thoughtful mouse was a diligent pupil who studied by candlelight every single night. As the years passed he became more knowledgeable about the world, more skilled as an orator and more objective in his reasoning. But for all of this, he felt more and more uncertain about the big cheese and whether he would ever find it. When he finally left the clever mouse and moved on to the next leg of this journey, he thanked the clever mouse for all that he had done for him, but moved on with a nagging feeling that he'd been wrong to stay for so very long.

The Lively Mouse and the Playful Mouse

The lively mouse set off before the crack of dawn and walked as far as he could before nightfall. By the end of the day, his little paws were sore, and his belly was rumbling. He was relieved when he saw a row of houses in the distance that stood alone overlooking the river below. The first house he came to was bright red, which set it apart from the rest of the street.

He knocked on the door and waited for an answer.

'Well hello!' exclaimed the playful mouse. 'What can I do for you?'

'I am on a journey, to find a big cheese in a faraway land. But my paws are sore and I am hungry,' he explained. 'Can I stay here for a night? I will gladly do any odd jobs that you have for me.'

The playful mouse threw its paws up into the air and pushed its chest out in a single movement. 'Tonight,' the mouse exclaimed, 'I am having a party. You really must join us. Tomorrow you can wash the glasses and all of the plates and help to tidy my little abode. But tonight, we celebrate!'

'Thank you,' said the lively mouse as they walked through into the living room.

The room was full to bursting with mice and cheese everywhere.

'Have some stilton,' smiled one of the guests, shaking crumbs out of his whiskers as he passed him a slice. 'There's also a very good brie in the corner.'

'Thank you,' said the lively mouse, filling his empty belly after spending the entire day walking.

'So,' asked his host, 'tell me more about this big cheese in a faraway land, sounds like quite the tall tale to me.'

'It's the biggest, tastiest cheese in the entire land,' he explained, 'and if I find it I will never go hungry again.'

'But we have plenty of good cheese here, you should let your hair down, relax, enjoy life a bit. You're only a young mouse once you know, you need to make the most of your youth while you can, eat, drink and be merry, laugh and enjoy yourself.'

'I'm sorry, but I have walked a very long way and I am tired. Tomorrow I have a long journey to go on and I would like to get some rest.'

'I'm the sensible mouse, and I have to be sensible or I'll never find my mysterious impossible cheese,' teased the playful mouse, pouting.

'And I'm the playful mouse,' the lively mouse replied, 'and I am the star of the show, I just thrive on the attention.'

The lively mouse stayed at the party longer than he felt he should, but he relaxed a bit and enjoyed himself, it had been a long time since he had been to a party and he enjoyed the company of the other mice. But when the clock struck midnight he made his excuses and went to bed and although the party kept going until sunrise, the lively mouse was so tired that he slept a deep, sound sleep.

The next morning he woke bright and early, just as the last guests were leaving and the playful mouse was heading to bed. There were crumbs of cheese everywhere and every dish in the house was piled up dirty on the kitchen stove.

The lively mouse scrubbed, scrubbed, scrubbed, all day long, so much so that it frayed the skin around his claws. He worked harder than he had ever worked before, saving what cheese could be saved, sweeping clean the floors and buffering the stove until it shone like a silver penny.

When the playful mouse finally woke, the sun was already going down.

'Wow, aren't you a good cleaner! This is the cleanest I think my house has ever been, won't you stay another night, tonight I think I'll have another party.'

'Thank you,' said the lively mouse, 'if I may I will stay one more night, but I will go to bed now as I am exhausted and tomorrow I will set off bright and early to continue my journey.'

'You really are a very curious little mouse aren't you,' replied the playful mouse, 'you really should have more fun you know.'

'I just have to continue my journey,' explained the lively mouse firmly.

'Well, there's no accounting for taste,' teased the playful mouse, 'but you have done an awfully good job today. Leave tomorrow morning if you wish and take some extra cheese for your journey, you've worked so very hard.'

'Thank you,' said the lively mouse gratefully, before scurrying off to bed.

It was dark when he got up the next morning and the playful mouse was still sleeping. He quickly washed the pans on the cooker and left a note to say goodbye before he left. He had a long journey ahead of him and the sun was just rising as he left.

The Thoughtful Mouse and the Playful Mouse

It was many years after the lively mouse that the thoughtful mouse encountered the playful mouse. He too came to the row of houses overlooking the river just as the sun was setting. His paws were sore from walking all day and his little tummy was rumbling.

He knocked on the door and waited for an answer.

'Well hello!' exclaimed the playful mouse. 'What can I do for you?'

'I am on a journey, to find a big cheese in a faraway land. But my paws are sore and I am hungry,' he explained. 'Can I stay here for a night? I will gladly do any odd jobs that you have for me.'

'Of course you can, come in, join the party,' said the playful mouse, 'and tomorrow you can clean up all of the plates and help to tidy my little pied-à-terre.'

'Thank you,' replied the lively mouse as they walked through into the living room which was once again full to bursting with mice gorging on cheese.

'Do you know anything about a big cheese, hidden somewhere in a faraway land?' the thoughtful mouse asked his host.

'There was another fellow I met many years ago now, who was also looking for the same cheese, but he was no fun and barely joined in at all. Won't you join the party? We have plenty of cheese here and then we can dance and swim in the river under the stars.'

The thoughtful mouse looked at the smile on his host's face and then around at all of the grinning mice around him and was quiet for a moment. Is the big cheese a metaphysical cheese after all and have these mice found it? They look so happy, surely there is something I can learn from them.

'Thank you,' the thoughtful mouse replied, 'I'd love to join your party, but I have to warn you, I'm not a very good dancer.'

'Then I shall teach you,' replied the playful mouse, 'I can teach you how to dress, etiquette, if you're lucky, I'll even share with you my best jokes and all of the juicy gossip I know about the other mice in the terrace.'

The thoughtful mouse ate more gouda, stilton and brie that night than he had ever done before, he talked and talked to the other mice and listened intently to what they had to say and although none of it related directly to the big cheese, he was having such a good time that he didn't really care.

As the night drew on, they danced and they danced until their little paws were red and then bathed them in the river, the warm summer waters soothing their tired bodies and washing the crumbs of cheese out of their fur. And as the thoughtful mouse stared up at the night's sky while he was swimming on his back, thinking about how small we are in a world lit up by so many stars, he thought that his quest was a foolish one and that he could do a lot worse than staying here for many more nights. After all, they seemed to have plenty of cheese already and they were all such happy mice.

The next morning when the thoughtful mouse woke up his head hurt so badly that he decided to go to sleep. It was only in the early evening, when the playful mouse woke him, that he got up and set about cleaning up after the party.

'We don't have much time to clean up,' the playful mouse said, 'I've already planned another party for later tonight.'

'I'm sorry I should have woken up earlier,' replied the thoughtful mouse.

'Oh no,' explained his host, 'it doesn't matter, we can just give everything a quick once over and clean everything more thoroughly tomorrow. Besides, cleaning isn't any fun anyway. Tonight, we'll have more cheese and dance and maybe take another refreshing swim in the river.'

This wasn't a one-off, however, over days and then weeks and then years this became the playful mouse and the thoughtful mouse's routine. Each night the thoughtful mouse would resolve to move on the next day and continue his search for the big cheese, but each night he would have such a good time and stare at the stars and feel so tiny and small that he would decide to stay for just one more day.

Over time the thoughtful mouse's fur began to thin and his belly grew fat from eating so much cheese, but his dancing improved and he learned to make all of the mice he met laugh and laugh until they couldn't laugh anymore. But something was missing. He felt even more confused now than when he had left the clever mouse and even more confused again than when he had left home.

One night, while swimming in the river after a particularly lively party, the thoughtful mouse remembered about the other mouse who'd set off on the same journey as him all of those years ago. How much further ahead was he? Had he already found the big cheese and if he had, would he be willing to share it with him? The thoughtful mouse didn't know the answers to these questions, but he was disappointed in himself for having wasted so much time and resolved that early tomorrow morning he would once again resume his journey and find the big cheese.

The Lively Mouse and the Busy Mouse

Once again the lively mouse walked until nightfall as he was anxious to progress on his journey and get ever closer to the big cheese. As the grey sky gradually turned to black, however, he began to worry about finding himself a bed for the night. Eventually, just as he was beginning to give up hope, he reached a strange, tall building, the tallest in fact that he had ever seen.

He knocked on the door and waited for an answer.

'What do you want?' asked the mouse that answered the door.

'I am on a journey, to find a big cheese in a faraway land. But my paws are sore and I am hungry,' he explained. 'Can I stay here for a night? I will gladly do any odd jobs that you have for me.'

The foremouse looked him up and down and then showed him into a huge room full of mice working every form of machinery imaginable. There were nuts everywhere – nuts being cracked, nuts being cleaned and nuts being packed into bags and the bags into boxes.

'Boss, this mouse wants to work here, but only for a day.'

The boss had a brusque manner to him and sharp, rat-like features. He was the busiest mouse the lively mouse had ever known, interrupting their conversation intermittently to give instructions to the other mice.

'We don't take on mice just for a day,' the busy mouse told him. 'If you want to work here you'll have to sign a contract. We'll need you to commit to working here for at least a month. But we offer full training and excellent opportunities for career progression.'

'But I am on a journey,' the lively mouse explained, 'to find a big cheese in a faraway land. This cheese is the biggest and tastiest cheese in the entire land and if I find it, I'll never go hungry again.'

'Fantasy, pure fantasy,' the busy mouse scoffed, 'besides I run the biggest nut processing company in the entire land. If you work here for a long time and work hard, you'll have your choice of nuts, pecans, pistachios, almonds, the lot.'

'But I prefer the taste of cheese,' the lively mouse explained, 'and I'm on a journey to find a very big cheese in a faraway land.'

'If you go into the city,' the busy mouse said, 'you'll be able to exchange the nuts you earn here for whatever kind of cheese you want. Don't waste your time on fantasies about finding a very big cheese, come and work here and we'll teach you everything you need to know about nuts and give you the opportunity to become one of the wealthiest mice in the land.'

'I'm very grateful for the opportunity sir,' said the lively mouse, 'but I'm not ready to give up my quest for the big cheese. How about I stay here for the night and tomorrow I work very hard for you, harder than I have ever worked before and then tomorrow you can pay me whatever you think my work is worth.'

'We are short-staffed sir,' said the foremouse, 'and there are some boxes of nuts that just need moving from the packing lines to the warehouse.'

'Very well,' said the busy mouse, before scurrying off to another appointment.

The lively mouse ate a simple dinner of peanuts that night and slept a long, deep sleep. The next morning, he woke at the crack of dawn and quickly set to work, shifting boxes of nuts on his back from the packing lines to the warehouse. The warehouse was in a separate building and the first journey took him twenty minutes, but by lunchtime he had figured out the best routes and perfected his technique, getting this down to only ten.

He barely stopped for lunch, eating only a few peanuts and worked until nightfall, when he could barely shift another box. His little paws were sore right through to the flesh and his back ached more than it had ever ached in his life.

The busy mouse spent only a few minutes inspecting his work.

'Excellent,' the busy mouse smiled, his two front teeth sticking out, 'you've clearly worked hard today. I'll happily pay you enough nuts for dinner plus some more to take on your way. But before you go, I just want to ask you one more time, won't you take up my offer of a job? A young mouse like you could have a real future here.'

'I'm sorry,' said the lively mouse, 'tomorrow I will continue my journey. It has only been a few days since I set off from home and I have much further to travel.'

'As you wish,' replied the busy mouse disappointed, 'but don't forget, there is a job offer here for you in the future if you want it.'

The lively mouse thanked him most graciously and once again slept a deep, peaceful sleep. He was exhausted and tomorrow he had a very long journey ahead of him.

The Thoughtful Mouse and the Busy Mouse

When he set off that morning, the thoughtful mouse was filled with expectation. But as the day wore on and his paws became sore and blistered, he began to realise just how lazy and out of shape he had become over the last few years. Despite this, he pushed on determined and just like the lively mouse he walked until nightfall until he came to a strange, tall building. It was the tallest, in fact, that he had ever seen.

He knocked on the door and waited for an answer.

'I am on a journey, to find a big cheese in a faraway land,' he explained to the foremouse, 'but my paws are sore and I am hungry. Can I stay here for a night? I will gladly do any odd jobs that you have for me.'

'I'll have to ask the boss,' the foremouse explained, showing him into the factory.

The thoughtful mouse looked around in awe at all of the other mice cleaning, cracking and packing nuts. He was hungry and he had never seen so many nuts in all of his life.

'So you want to work here? But only for a day?' The busy mouse demanded.

'Yes sir, you see I am on a journey to find a big cheese in a faraway land, but I am hungry and need a place to stay for the night. I will happily work all day tomorrow in return for bed and board.'

The busy mouse looked him up and down, appraising his fitness for work, dwelling on his round flabby belly.

'I can offer you a job, but you'll need to join our training program which takes a month,' the busy mouse explained, smiling through his big rat-like teeth.

'But I'm on a journey, I only want to stay here for a short while, I still want to find the big cheese,' the thoughtful mouse repeated.

'I run the biggest nut processing company in the land. Forget about your fantasy of finding a big cheese. Besides, we have as many nuts here as you could possibly eat. You'll have your choice of nuts, pecans, pistachios, almonds, the lot.'

The thoughtful mouse was quiet while he reflected on whether to take the offer of a job. Only last night he had resolved to continue his quest for the big cheese, perhaps he should walk on just a bit further and find somewhere he could stay for just a night. But his belly was rumbling and his feet were very sore.

The busy mouse seemed to read what he was thinking.

'If you go into the city,' the busy mouse said, 'you'll be able to exchange the nuts you earn here for whatever kind of cheese you want,' he told him. 'Don't waste your time on fantasies about finding a very big cheese, come and work here and we'll teach you everything you need to know about nuts and give you the opportunity to become one of the wealthiest mice in the land.'

The busy mouse seemed very impatient while the thoughtful mouse considered his offer, despite busying himself with giving orders to all of the other mice while he was waiting.

The big cheese was about more than cheese itself. During his time with the clever mouse the thoughtful mouse had realised that it could be a metaphorical cheese, but he also wanted to find a real big cheese, somewhere, if not in a distant land than in this one. He felt confused, he was still on a journey but now he was unsure of its goal, he had only hazy memories of its beginning and wasn't entirely sure if the journey was really worth the effort. But staying here didn't seem to make much sense either.

'I can tell you are having second thoughts,' the busy mouse said, cracking open a nut with his huge teeth, 'you should still go and find your big cheese, but join our training program and you'll learn everything you need to find it. Going on a long journey like that is a lot like running a vast enterprise like mine, you need to be able to organise things just so, or otherwise the whole endeavour falls over. Stay here for a month or two and then see how you feel.'

'Okay,' conceded the thoughtful mouse, who didn't really know enough about the nut processing industry to know that it really didn't have that much to do with cheese.

The next day the thoughtful mouse started on the training course and over the next month he learnt all about inspecting nuts, cracking nuts, cleaning nuts and packing them. But it wasn't just him on the training course, he was one of a cohort of thirty mice and there would be another thirty mice joining behind them in just six months.

Initially, the thoughtful mouse prevaricated. He thought almost every day about leaving the nut processing company and resuming his search for the big cheese, particularly as he was paid just a single peanut each day during his apprenticeship. But he'd been promised that once he completed the training program, he'd receive a handful of peanuts each day and that if he progressed further, he had the chance to earn more nuts than he had ever wanted.

The nut plant was a very hierarchical company and there was much infighting amongst the mice trying to progress to the next level. At the lowest level were the nutcrackers – this was really paw-breaking labour that took all of your energy but wasn't particularly skilled. At the highest level were the managers and supervisors, but the thoughtful mouse wasn't entirely sure what they did, other than shouting at the mice doing all the work every so often and running around squealing to each other.

Despite this, the thoughtful mouse worked harder than he had ever worked before, if his peers cracked one hundred nuts in a day, he cracked a hundred and ten and when they progressed to cracking two hundred nuts in a day, he cracked two hundred and fifty. Despite this, the busy mouse was reluctant to promote him.

'You're not quite ready yet,' he would smile his rat-like grin, 'keep at it though and I'm sure you'll progress in time.'

This angered the thoughtful mouse and he once again thought about leaving and resuming his search for the big cheese. But he was a determined young mouse who didn't like to be beaten, so he worked even harder, so that his paws were sore from cracking nuts at the end of every single day.

Eventually, he was promoted and he was paid a single walnut each day, alongside his peanuts. Initially, this seemed like a big deal, waiting as he had for the promotion for so very long. And over time, day after day eating walnuts, he acquired a real taste for them, even if they weren't quite as tasty as cheese. After a few months though, he thought once again about quitting and resuming his quest for the big cheese, but he'd been working so hard that he wasn't quite sure what the big cheese was anymore and why it had once mattered to him so very much.

The thoughtful mouse was fascinated by the busy mouse, who seemed to have more nuts than he knew what to do with and did everything he could to try to impress him. Over time, he started to emulate the managers and the supervisors that had found favour with the busy mouse and tried to be as like them as possible. They were all very busy mice and over time the thoughtful mouse stopped being such a thoughtful mouse and instead, he himself became a very busy mouse as well.

Soon he found himself being much more political and calculated about what he had to say. He'd take credit for other mice's ideas and blame other mice when things went wrong. This seemed to work and eventually he was promoted to a supervisory position. Then he started to tell all of the mice that worked for him that they too had a bright future with the company, way ahead of all of their young competitors, provided they worked hard and gave things their all.

The years wore on and the progressively busier and progressively less thoughtful mouse progressed in his career and became more and more distant not only from the big cheese but also from the young, idealistic mouse who'd set off on a journey all of those years ago. But something was missing, deep down inside him and even though he now had his choice of nuts, he found himself wandering into the city each night and exchanging his hard-earned nuts for every type of cheese imaginable. But despite buying the most expensive Gruyère and Morbier he could find, it never tasted as good as he hoped and he began to wonder whether any type of cheese, whether the big cheese or any other type of cheese could ever really make him happy.

He became progressively more depressed and self-indulgent. His fur began to fall out and his whole underside became a big, flabby belly from binging on too many nuts. He became harsher with everyone in his life, but also more insecure. Outwardly he projected an image of confidence that he had spent the last few years perfecting from copying other mice, but inwardly he felt unbalanced. He felt as if he had been deceived, but he couldn't quite put his paw on exactly how.

After one particularly long day, where he'd worked a good eighteen hours resolving issues with buyers and suppliers and dealing with a breakdown on one of the nut-cracking lines, he flew into a terrible rage. It was like something had snapped within him and he had lost the self-control, the self-deception that he had spent all of the last few years perfecting.

He marched into the busy mouse's office, interrupting him in the middle of a gouda sandwich.

'You told me working here would help me to find the big cheese,' he said, adopting a rather accusatory tone.

The busy mouse put down his sandwich and smiled his rat-like smile, crumbs falling out of his whiskers as he did so.

'I told you what you needed to hear,' he replied.

'It was a lie,' the thoughtful mouse snarled, surprising himself with his frankness.

'It's the same lie you've been telling all of the mice that now work for you,' the busy mouse replied, in the same matter of fact tone he used when discussing the monthly figures.

'So you don't think there's anything more to a mouse's life than just accumulating as many nuts as possible?' the thoughtful mouse demanded.

'I can see you've had a difficult day,' said the busy mouse, conspicuously adopting a more concerned tone, 'why don't you take a holiday, I'm sure we can manage without you for a few weeks. All work and no play makes Jack a dull mouse. Besides, it's spring in the Alps, cheese fondue, some skiing, you'll be back to your old self in no time!'

'You've treated me like a mouse in a maze,' he replied, 'always laying out a little trail of nuts to make me go exactly where you wanted.'

'No,' replied the busy mouse, 'I only offered you opportunities, I never forced you to stay against your will.'

'But I was only going to stay for a short while,' protested the thoughtful mouse, 'and I ended up wasting most of my life here.'

'We've fed thousands, maybe even millions of mice in the time that you've worked here,' replied the busy mouse, 'how can you call that a waste?'

'But only with nuts!' shouted the thoughtful mouse, 'Never with cheese.' But as the words left his mouth, he knew that his time at the nut processing plant had come to an end and that tomorrow, he would once again resume his search for the big cheese.

The Lively Mouse and the Political Mouse

Once again, the lively mouse set off at sunrise and as he walked further from the nut factory, the landscape became greener and the buildings became more sparse. It was not until the sun was beginning to set that he began to look for a place to stay for the night.

Given how rural the landscape was it took him a long time before he finally reached a small, thatched cottage that reminded him of the cottage he had stayed in on that very first night away from home.

He knocked on the door and waited for an answer.

'Who are you?' said the long-haired mouse that opened the door. 'Who do you represent?'

'I am on a journey, to find a big cheese in a faraway land. But my paws are sore and I am hungry,' he explained once again. 'Can I stay here for a night? I will gladly do any odd jobs that you have for me.'

'Come in, come in,' the political mouse greeted him warmly, 'we have much to discuss.'

The inside of the cottage was much like the clever mouse's cottage. It too was piled high with books, but the walls were crammed full of pictures of mice with big rosettes pinned to their fur looking very pleased with themselves.

'So do you have work for me?' the lively moused asked.

'Help yourself to some cheese,' the political mouse said, 'cutting him a slice of Edam. I am running for election and I need someone to distribute all of my pamphlets to the local electorate. Tomorrow, you can help me with canvassing, but you shouldn't do it just for board and lodging, you see what this land of ours needs is proper leadership. The current mouse council just isn't getting things right.'

'I'm not interested in politics,' explained the lively mouse, 'I'm on a journey to a faraway land in search of the big cheese.'

'No, no, no!' replied the political mouse, in much the same tone as the clever mouse, 'You're going about this completely wrong. You won't be able to find the big cheese on your own. You'll need to assemble a group of like-minded mice, an expeditionary force who can work together to find the big cheese. Endeavours of this size need to be organised on the societal level; no meaningful change is ever accomplished by a single individual.'

'I'm most grateful for your hospitality and I will gladly help you to distribute your pamphlets,' replied the lively mouse firmly, 'but the day after tomorrow I will leave because this is a journey I have to take on my own.'

'Then you will surely fail in your endeavour,' replied the political mouse, cutting himself another slice of Edam, 'don't be so hasty, let's analyse the problem. You would like to find the big cheese, a cheese so big that if you find it you will never go hungry again. But if it's that big, you could surely share it with many other mice and still have more cheese than you could ever eat left over. But finding the cheese is a difficult endeavour, so it's only logical you would look to your fellow mice for help, isn't it?'

'Perhaps you are right,' the lively mouse conceded, 'but I have barely been travelling for a few days, perhaps, if further into my journey I feel the need for help, I will do as you suggest, but as things stand, at the moment, I just want to keep travelling and see how far I can get on my own.'

'As you wish,' replied the political mouse, flicking Edam from his whiskers in irritation, 'but I want you to know that you are being selfish and that you are depriving society of the big cheese.'

'But it's quite possible that no one will ever find it,' mused the lively mouse, 'besides I am only a single mouse, how much of an impact can I really have?'

'The young mice of today,' the political mouse lamented, shaking his head.

'Do you mind if I take an early night,' the lively mouse excused himself, 'I have walked a long way today and I will have a busy day tomorrow.'

'Okay,' the political mouse sighed, 'although I am disappointed you don't want to talk more about the issues that matter.'

The next day the lively mouse scurried all over the county distributing the political mouse's pamphlets. He wasn't really sure what they were all about, but he wasn't really interested anyway, his focus was on finding the big cheese. By the end of the day, his little paws were sore and he was tired, so he ate a little cheese, made his excuses and went to bed.

The next day he set off once again on his quest for the big cheese. But he felt a growing apprehension about his journey as if all of the other mice knew something that he didn't and they hadn't yet let him in on the joke.

The Thoughtful Mouse and the Political Mouse

When the thoughtful mouse left the nut factory that morning, he set off with a spring in his step and feeling lighter in his soul. He was leaving behind a life that he had come to hate and a whole mess of intractable problems. He was now a much older mouse, but despite everything that had happened to him over the years, he still believed something was missing in his life. He was determined to find the big cheese, whatever that meant and wherever that quest would take him.

He had grown out of shape during his years at the nut factory and his paws were quick to blister and his little legs soon felt tired under the weight of his belly. But despite this, he kept scurrying along on his way and despite the physical discomfort, he actually enjoyed the walk. As he walked further into the countryside and the sun began to sink behind the fields, he approached a small, thatched cottage that reminded him of the clever mouse's house.

He knocked on the door and waited for an answer.

'Who are you?' said the long-haired mouse that opened the door. 'Who do you represent?'

'I am on a journey, to find a big cheese in a faraway land. But my paws are sore and I am hungry,' he explained once again. 'Can I stay here for a night? I will gladly do any odd jobs that you have for me.'

'Come in, come in,' the political mouse greeted him warmly, 'we have much to discuss.'

The thoughtful mouse looked around at all of the books and couldn't help but feel a nagging nostalgia for all of the time that he had spent studying all of those years ago.

'Would you like some gouda?' asked the political mouse.

'Yes please,' he replied sitting down in front of the fire, 'I'd gladly do some work in exchange for some food and a place to stay.'

'Yes, yes, we'll get to all of that,' replied the political mouse with a grin, 'but first of all, tell me about this very big cheese of yours.'

'Well sir,' replied the thoughtful mouse, 'one day, when I was just a young mouse, an old man came to our village and told me about a very big cheese in a faraway land. It's the biggest, tastiest cheese in the entire world and if I can find it I will never go hungry again.'

'Is this cheese big enough to feed a village, a county, maybe even the whole country?'

'I don't know, it might be, I still need to find the cheese.'

'Don't you see,' said the political mouse excitedly, 'this big cheese could solve all of our problems, we could feed every mouse in the entire land.'

'But first we'd have to find the big cheese,' lamented the thoughtful mouse, 'I've been searching for it for my entire life and I am no closer now to finding it than when I started this journey many, many years ago.'

'If you don't mind me saying,' said the political mouse peering over his reading glasses and looking him directly in the eye, 'you haven't found it because you've been going about this completely the wrong way. A project as big as this can only be achieved by a group of us together. It's a big project, we literally need to search the entire land.'

'But I am only a single mouse,' lamented the thoughtful mouse.

'Don't you worry! I have a plan. Tomorrow we can put posters up all over the county to promote our cause. We'll recruit a whole army of like-minded mice to help search for the big cheese. We will find it, you mark my words, together we can achieve anything.'

True to his word, the next morning the political mouse printed hundreds of posters and they travelled all over the county putting them up. They stuck them to buildings, trees, even the tarmac of the road, they put posters almost everywhere and before long all of the mice in the county were squeaking about the very big cheese and the meeting the next day to discuss it.

For the first time in a long while the thoughtful mouse felt optimistic about finding the big cheese and when he went to bed that night, he could barely sleep for his excitement. Nevertheless, the next day eventually came and when he woke up that morning, there were already mice assembling in the political mouse's front room.

When the start of the meeting finally came around, there were so many mice that they had to move outside into a field to fit all of them in. The political mouse perched on a bail of straw and greeted them all with enthusiasm.

'Brothers and sisters,' he squealed, 'I have brought us all together today to right the wrongs of the recent past and to unite us all, each and every mouse regardless of where they were born or the colour of their fur, behind a shared future of prosperity. There is,' he paused for dramatic effect, 'somewhere,' he paused again, 'a very big cheese and if we find this cheese we will never go hungry again. I say let us all unite, together we can find it and begin a new era of brotherhood and prosperity the likes of which we have never known.'

'Point of order, point of order!' yelled a very furry grey mouse from the back, 'I'm all for finding this big cheese, but why should you lead us. For an endeavour as big as this, you need experienced leadership, someone like me who really knows his cheese.'

The mice surrounding the furry grey mouse all started to squeak excitedly in support.

'You may know your cheese,' replied the political mouse, sounding irritated, 'but there's more to life than cheese. We need a leader who knows this land and the mice who live in it, who can help us search for the cheese but also to ensure that it is shared fairly once we find it.'

The mice around the political mouse also squealed in support.

'So you're saying,' the furry grey mouse replied, raising his voice, 'that those mice that do the most to find the big cheese should get the same share as those mice who do nothing?'

'That's not what I'm saying and you know it,' replied the political mouse, 'I'm merely saying that any division of the cheese must be equitable and serve the wider interests of society as a whole.'

The two mice went on and on arguing like this, but for some strange reason that the thoughtful mouse didn't quite understand their animosity towards each other seemed to be contagious. Soon enough the mice in the crowd were biting on each other's tails and scratching at each other's paws.

They argued and they argued and they argued. At first for hours and then for days. The thoughtful mouse watched all of this with a great deal of patience, perhaps this was how any great endeavour involving any large task force of mice had to be organised, after all, you needed to agree on things before you could all work together. But as the long hours of debate wore on the thoughtful mouse became more and more depressed.

Finally, on the third day, he built up the courage to speak.

'Excuse me!' he said. 'Excuse me but I just want to say that we're never going to find the big cheese like this, we need to make a plan for how we'll find it. So far, all we've done is argued about how we'll divide the big cheese once we get it, but surely before that, we all need to figure out a plan to find it.'

'Bravo,' said the political mouse with a wry smile, 'of course we need to figure out a plan to find the big cheese. I say let's start planning right away, who's with me?'

'Stop right there,' declared the furry grey mouse, 'I say we start planning right away as well, who is with me?'

'Don't let him fool you,' the political mouse warned, 'do you really want to follow him on a quest to find the big cheese only for him to take the biggest share for himself once you find it!'

'Do you really think his expedition will even succeed,' his opponent retorted, 'given how he plans to organise things. Why would any mouse work hard to even find it? No, follow me,' he declared, 'and we will find the big cheese before them!'

But although each of the two mice said there and then that they would set off on the expedition, neither of them did. Instead, they stayed exactly where they were and tried to win as many mice as possible over to their side. Before long a third mouse joined in and then a fourth and then a fifth. They spilt into fractions and then fractions within fractions.

As the days wore on and then the years, the thoughtful mouse listened to each of the mice in turned and tried to decide who to follow. He felt a loyalty to the political mouse who had started all of this, but then he prevaricated and then he changed his mind again. Each time he felt excited, like the mouse he was listening to was right and that he could believe what they were saying, but each time he moved on to listen to a different mouse he learnt that what he had previously been told was wrong.

Eventually, he began not to trust what any of the mice were saying. One night, when the mice were arguing late into the evening and the bright red sun was dropping tired behind the edges of the cornfield, he thought back to all of the mice that he had met along his journey and all of the things that they had told him. Were they all the same, the clever mouse, the playful mouse, the busy mouse and even all of these political mice? Was there really anything to what any of them had to say?

Without saying goodbye and without making a scene, he scurried off towards the sinking red sun that looked like it was falling off the end of the world and ran until his little paws were too tired to carry him any further. He didn't know where he was running to, but he just knew he had to get away.

The Lively Mouse and the Thoughtful Mouse

When the thoughtful mouse started walking again the next morning, he felt like he was walking away from his past, from the clever mouse, the playful mouse, the busy mouse and the political mouse, but he had no idea where he was going. The big cheese now seemed like everything and nothing, something which by its very nature was impossible to find.

He was done with taking the advice of other mice and when nightfall came he refused to look for shelter, but instead lay down on his belly and slept under the stars. He carried on like this for several nights, becoming hungrier, thirstier and more full of regrets.

On the fourth day, a bright red disk pushed its way unstoppably over the horizon, took its place in the clear sky and warmed the skin under his fur. He has lost any sense of place and was simply wandering through the countryside with no aim in mind. His wandering within himself was the walk that he was taking and if physical movement somehow made that easier, then he would move.

He walked for miles and miles without finding even a puddle from which to drink, the dust of the road clogging up his throat and his paws becoming heavy like lead. It was not until late in the day, under the heat of the evening sun that he thought he could hear water and as he drew closer, he realised he was approaching a brook.

He stopped in his tracks and stared at the mouse before him.

His eyes, nose and whiskers were so like those of the mouse he had known in his childhood, the very same mouse who had left on the same quest for the big cheese all of those years ago. And yet his face had a blankness to it, had lost its hope and expectancy.

He smiled at him and waited for a reaction as the other mouse appeared to be appraising him in much the same way.

'Brother,' the thoughtful mouse ventured.

'Brother,' the lively mouse replied.

He paused before he continued. 'You look exhausted, please drink from the brook, refresh yourself.'

'I've come so far,' the thoughtful mouse sighed.

'Haven't we both,' replied the lively mouse.

The thoughtful mouse drank his fill of water and then they sat together, under a willow tree, their paws dangling in cool water, watching the gnats dance over the surface.

They exchanged stories of their travels and all of the different mice that they had met. The lively mouse had moved faster than the thoughtful mouse, but he'd met the same kind of mice as the thoughtful mouse along his way.

They sat in silence together for a long time before the thoughtful mouse broke the silence.

'Brother, I have wasted my life. I have been too easily led by others, I have lost track of my quest and am no closer to finding the big cheese than when I left home all of those years ago.'

To his surprise, the lively mouse laughed. 'Brother,' he confided, 'I have wasted my life. I have been so set on finding the big cheese that I haven't stopped along the way to enjoy myself or to listen to others. What will you do now?' the lively mouse asked.

'One thing is for sure, I'm going to spend less time listening to everyone else and more time listening to me. I'm not sure if I even believe in the big cheese anymore, but I sure know what I don't believe in. I don't believe in studying just to be able to bamboozle other mice, I don't believe in being playful just for the sake of pretending I don't feel any emptiness, I don't believe in keeping busy just to accumulate nuts or to distract me from myself and I don't believe in forming a committee to try to solve the problem of the mouse condition.'

'That's all very well,' the lively mouse replied gravely, 'but where will you go next, what will you actually do?'

'I don't know yet,' he sighed, 'perhaps you have a better idea than me.'

'Brother, I have been free to wander these lands and I have seen more of the world than most mice see in a lifetime. I have worked hard but I have always kept on the move. I have met so many different mice, but I've never really got to know them, I've never been willing to let them distract me from finding the big cheese, I've always been wary of mouse traps.'

'So did you find the big cheese?' the thoughtful mouse asked hopefully.

'I am no closer to finding the big cheese than you brother,' he laughed a sad, tired laugh, 'but I know loneliness, I know what happens when a mouse crawls so deep within his own soul that he can't see any way out.'

'Do you feel lonely now?' asked the thoughtful mouse.

'No,' the lively mouse smiled, 'right now I feel listened to, I feel I am with a kindred mouse.'

'So why do you need to ever feel lonely again?'

The lively mouse let out a long, pained laugh. 'Why do you need to feel like you've wasted your life? Think of everything that you have learned, all of the mice that you have known. You don't have to turn your back on that just because you're going to start listening to yourself more as well.'

'Do you know what,' the thoughtful mouse said, 'perhaps between us both, we have found the big cheese after all.'

'Cheese is all around us,' the lively mouse smiled, 'I don't know why I got so obsessed with finding a big one in the first place really. Do you?'

Epilogue

The lively mouse and the thoughtful mouse travelled together for some months, stopping to take shelter in exchange for work along the way. Encouraged by his brother, the lively mouse spent more time talking to other mice and listened to what they had to say without obsessing over the big cheese. He became more open to others and less intent on searching for a mythical solution to life. Encouraged by the lively mouse, the thoughtful mouse became more in touch with himself and his inner mouse, he became more vocal about his needs and less easily led by others. Eventually, both mice agreed that they were tired of travelling and they headed back to the village in which they were born.

The lively mouse became the centre of the community. He built an inn where any mouse could stop and get a good meal and a bed for the night. The thoughtful mouse became the wise mouse of the village, running the village school and then starting a small college. Both mice met someone and settled down. About 20 days later, they became fathers.

Once a year on the anniversary of setting off on their quests all of those years ago, they would go to the local cheesemongers and buy a very big cheese and share it with the village. 'Cheese is all around us,' they would toast and both of them would laugh at their folly. But both of them were happy and both of them knew, deep down, that without the journeys that they had been on they wouldn't be the happy mice that they are today.

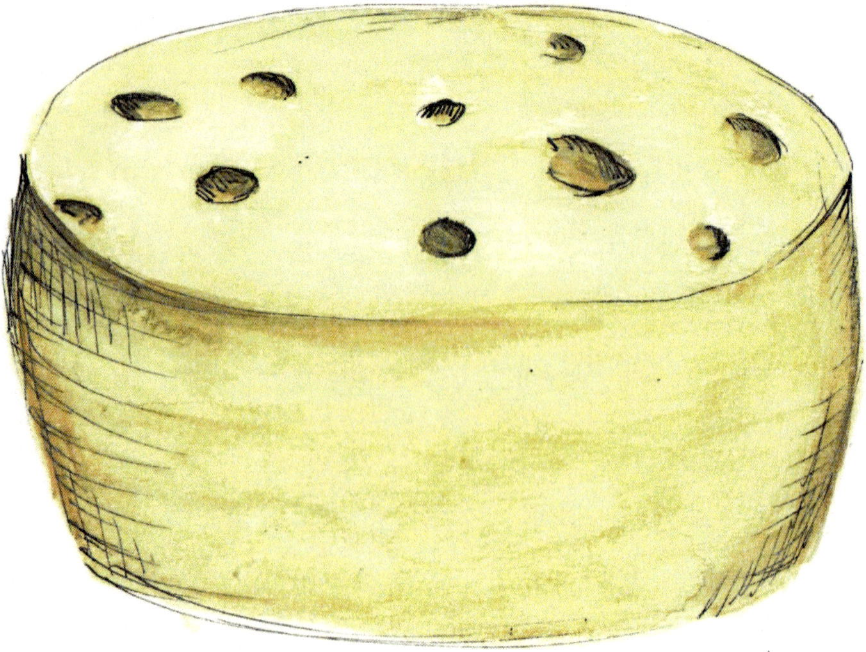